WAREHAM
A Pictorial History

Aerial view, looking towards Northport, *c*.1950. The town is snugly enclosed within the Saxon walls. On the right the parish church of Lady St Mary dominates the townscape. In the distance is Northport, a small hamlet which grew dramatically after the railway arrived in 1847.

WAREHAM
A Pictorial History

Lilian Ladle

Phillimore

1994

Published by
PHILLIMORE & CO. LTD.,
Shopwyke Manor Barn, Chichester, Sussex

ISBN 0 85033 900 6

Printed and bound in Great Britain by
BIDDLES LTD.,
Guildford, Surrey

To
Martin Ayres

List of Illustrations

Frontispiece: Wareham, looking towards Northport, *c.*1950

Acknowledgements

This book would not have been possible without Ken Ayres who has so ably reproduced all the photographic material. Martin Ayres, despite pending examinations, has devoted considerable time to the project.

Thanks are extended to Harry Clark and Mick O'Hara for stimulating conversation regarding Wareham and to Jon and Rosemarie Hall for reading the text. Lastly, thanks to my husband Mike, who has constantly encouraged me in my efforts to record Wareham's past.

I am most grateful to Carole O'Hara for the line drawings 1, 172, and to Hugh Jaques of the Dorset County Record Office for use of the following reproductions 2, 32, 34, 41.

Gratitude is owed to all the following owners of photographs who gave permission to use their material: Martin Ayres, 11, 12, 17, 35-37, 47, 50, 53, 54, 58, 60, 79, 95, 96, 102, 103, 111, 115, 120, 126, 131, 133, 137, 140, 141, 147; Ken Ayres, 23, 39, 48, 109, 123, 171; Monty Best, 3, 4, 8, 30, 31, 66, 97, 108, 114, 139, 146; Dave Burt, 105; Harry Clark, 15, 110; Keith Critchley, 144; Betty Dugdale, 143; Graham Elmes, 112, 113, 130, 163, 164, 166; Hugh Elmes, 6, 21, 27-29, 51, 52, 65, 74, 94, 136, 157, 167; Canon Peter Hardman and the Parochial Church Council of Lady St Mary, 33; Roy Hillman, 5, 9, 19, 43, 46, 62, 67, 70-73, 76, 84, 86, 88, 89, 100, 101, 117, 119, 124, 129, 132, 138, 149, 151, 156, 159-161; Mike Ladle, 49, 55, 57; Hetty Simmonds, 10, 20, 40, 78, 80, 90, 169; Jack Spiller, 25, 26; Eileen Stuckey, 165, 168; Fred Toms, 106, Ray Watkins, 158; Wareham Museum, Frontispiece, 16, 22, 24, 42, 63, 56, 77, 81, 83, 91-93, 104, 118, 121, 125, 127, 128, 142, 155, 162, 170; The following photographs are from the author's collection, 7, 13, 14, 18, 38, 44, 45, 59, 61, 64, 68, 69, 75, 82, 85, 87, 98, 99, 107, 116, 122, 134, 135, 145, 148, 150, 152-154.

Any errors or omissions are the sole responsibility of the author.

Introduction

Prehistoric Beginnings

The small Dorset town of Wareham has a long and chequered past which spans two thousand years. Its development has been affected in turn by the Roman occupation, an early Saxon church, Viking invasions, two civil wars and a calamitous fire. The story can be read in its buildings, monuments and streets as well as on the pages of history books.

In the beginning some seven or eight thousand years ago, hunter-gatherers roamed the margins of Poole harbour. Their beautifully worked flint tools are occasionally found—our only evidence of the first inhabitants. By the Bronze Age, men had settled in this part of Purbeck and although their dwelling sites have yet to be located, to the north and west of the town, their burial sites survive in profusion.

On the eve of the Roman invasion in A.D. 43 Purbeck was a patchwork of small settlements, many of them utilising the natural resources of clay, stone, chalk and shale. This wealth of minerals ensured that the area was very quickly developed and exploited for the benefit of the Roman empire. It is likely that the earliest settlers in what was to become the town of Wareham, were subsistence farmers who occupied land in the West Walls area. Evidence in the form of pits, pots and the clay floors of their buildings was discovered during excavations on the western ramparts in 1952. Artefacts from this period have been found all over the town but most finds have been concentrated in the north-west quadrant. A mile to the east of Wareham at Swineham Point on the Bestwall peninsula, at the harbour's edge, there was a substantial settlement surrounded by ditches and enclosures.

When the Romans arrived, pottery making was a well-established industry. To the west of Wareham at Worgret, a large pottery producing site was operational for four centuries. It seems likely that the native potters had won military contracts very early in the first century. Their pots, the dark shiny dishes, jars, cooking pots, plates and flagons now known as 'Black Burnished ware' were in great demand by the army and are found all over Britain in places occupied by the legions. The site was 'accidentally' discovered by another military presence— the British Army in 1917. Kilns have also been found at nearby Stoborough and Ridge.

The location of Wareham was well chosen. The south-facing land between the rivers Frome and Piddle was ideally situated for a growing settlement and the Frome, in particular, gave access to a fertile hinterland. A road system was quickly established with links south to the industrial sites of Purbeck, north to Bere and Badbury and west to the *civitas* capital of Durnovaria (Dorchester). Wareham's status was probably that of a small market centre with port facilities. During building work at Northport in 1989, a number of skeletons were unearthed. It seems likely that a small cemetery developed beside the northern road out of the town. Only one body was excavated; it was lying east-west and without grave goods— possibly this burial was Christian.

Early in the fifth century when the Romans left Britain, the country experienced a sudden and total 'systems' collapse. The money-based economy which had driven the province for the previous four centuries was no longer in operation after the withdrawal of the legions. The natives quickly reverted to subsistence farming and barter—the way of life of their Iron-age ancestors.

The Homestead by the Weir

Wareham is one of the few places where there is strong evidence of occupation during the 'Dark Ages'. Last century, when the nave of the parish church was demolished, five crudely carved inscribed stones were found incorporated into the fabric of the building. They were the gravestones of Celtic Christians, four men and a woman, who had lived and worshipped in the area in the seventh and eighth centuries. The names were inscribed on pieces of Roman masonry, which no doubt had come from a building of some status; however, its identity and location remain a mystery. Memorials such as these are unknown in this part of the country but occur with some frequency in the West Country and Wales. It would seem likely that the stones belonged to a monastic community in Wareham which was flourishing before the Saxons were established in the area in the 650s.

Local legend recalls that in about 700 St Aldhelm, first bishop of the West Saxons, founded a nunnery and an imposing stone-built church on the banks of the Frome. This 'minster' church would have served most of the present Purbeck area and later medieval parishes were carved out of this large tract of land. A lay community developed outside the convent precinct and it was from these beginnings that the modern town of Wareham grew.

The place is noted in the Anglo-Saxon Chronicle in 786 as 'Werham'—the homestead by the weir. By then the 'homestead' had developed into an important settlement and the weir would have been a fish trap set across the river Frome to catch salmon and eels. The salmon fishery has a long history and the Frome is still one of the country's best known salmon fishing rivers.

In 802, Beorhtric, king of the West Saxons, was buried in the convent church. He had been married to Eadburh, daughter of the legendary Offa of Mercia. However, as she was unable to dominate the court as she wished, she murdered many of her husband's followers by poison and ended up by killing Beorhtric in the same way. Several years later the king's body was re-buried in Tewkesbury Abbey. It is likely that the royal residence lay close to, if not in, Wareham itself.

Alfred's Fortified Town

Tremendous problems beset the English kingdoms of Wessex, Mercia, East Anglia and Northumbria in the ninth century. Raiding bands from Scandinavia attacked the country with increasing frequency, causing chaos and havoc. The kings of Northumbria and East Anglia were murdered, the king of Mercia fled to Rome, and only Alfred of Wessex stood in the way of the threatened Viking domination of all England. By 876, the Viking army had moved overland from Cambridge to Wareham and there they were joined by a ship-borne force. Alfred quickly gathered his forces together and surrounded the town, where up to 2,000 Vikings were beleaguered. King Alfred made a treaty with this 'host' and, despite promises of peace and a speedy departure from his kingdom, hostages were killed and the army escaped under cover of darkness to Exeter. Meanwhile a reputed 120 ships of the Viking navy were lost in a storm off Swanage.

Asser, Alfred's chronicler and personal monk, gives us the first written description of Wareham: 'Situated between the rivers Frome and Tarrant, in a very secure position except in the west where it is joined to the mainland'. The nuns and convent are mentioned and the town is termed a 'castellum' or fortified place.

Alfred's policy of strengthening strategic and major settlements dated from this period and there are strong grounds for believing that Wareham's defensive walls had been constructed before the Vikings invaded. The town's importance at this time can be deduced from the 'Burghal Hidage', a document compiled in the early 900s. Wareham was the fourth largest town in Wessex; only Winchester, the royal capital, and Wallingford and Southwark both on the vulnerable Mercian borders were larger. The earthen ramparts which surrounded the town on three sides were 2,200 yards in extent and 1,600 men were required to defend and maintain them. It would seem that the rectilinear street pattern was set at this time.

When Edward (the Martyr) came to the throne, Wareham was a thriving market town with the royal privilege of minting its own coin. After his murder at Corfe in 978, the king's body was interred at the convent church. However, once again the royal burial was lost when in 980 the relics were conveyed with great ceremony to Shaftesbury Abbey. Donations at St Edward's shrine ensured that the abbey became one of the richest in the country. That same year the death of Wareham's last abbess, Wulfwyn, was recorded in the Anglo-Saxon Chronicle; the days of the nunnery were numbered. Its church Lady St Mary was given by Edward the Confessor to the French abbey of Fontanelle and a cell of canons installed. The king's holiness and his mother's Norman ancestry were likely reasons for the gift.

Before the Norman conquest, there were also two other churches in the town, St Martin's at the north gate and St Andrew's guarding the river crossing in the south. Their founding dates are unknown but both parishes were very large, extending many miles beyond the walls. It is possible that timber buildings preceded the erection of stone churches on these sites. St Andrew's was a possession of Horton Abbey, near Wimborne—later, ownership was transferred to Sherborne Abbey. Excavations at St Martin's in 1986 raised the possibility of a building beneath the present church. There is a local tradition that the first church was destroyed by Cnut during a raid up the Frome in 1015. After his accession to the English throne and conversion to Christianity, the church was reputedly rebuilt.

Conquest, Castles and Civil War

When William the Norman conquered England in 1066, Wareham was Dorset's largest borough with nearly three hundred houses and an estimated population of over a thousand. Two mints had been producing coinage, a simple silver penny, for 150 years. By the time that Domesday Book was compiled in 1086, 130 dwellings had vanished; many no doubt had been razed to allow a castle to be built in the south-west corner of the town. This monumental survey noted the nearby settlement at Bestwall, a productive manor with the only recorded woodland in the locality. Also mentioned were Worgret and Stoborough, small farming hamlets with access to mills on the river Frome.

No sooner had the town adjusted to and recovered from the changes wrought by the conquest, than it was involved in another conflict. Between 1135 and 1153 the country was plunged into civil war while the Conqueror's grandchildren, Stephen and Matilda, battled for the throne. As a cross-channel port with strong Norman links, Wareham's position was both important and vulnerable. The castle, which overlooked the Frome, was a royal residence as well as a state prison and garrison, and during the conflict it changed hands nine times. On a number of occasions the town suffered greatly. In 1137, after seizing the castle, Stephen set the town on fire as a punishment to the townsmen for rallying to Matilda. St Andrew's church, just outside the castle precinct, is thought to have been so badly damaged during the fighting that complete rebuilding was necessary. With the new church went a new dedication to the Holy Trinity.

After the war, Wareham castle fell from favour; the royal purse spent lavishly on Corfe Castle three miles to the south, which had survived this period of turmoil unscathed, its superior defensive position making it virtually impregnable. Although Wareham's castle has long since gone, Pound Lane and West Street still respect the curve of the inner and outer baileys of the Norman stronghold.

The priory church, which had avoided damage during the war, was extended at the beginning of the 12th century by the addition of St Edward's chapel, built next to the chancel. Here, shafts of Purbeck marble support the stone roof. It was one of the first parish churches to use this stone in such a way. The church also acquired a magnificent decorated lead font at this time. In 1150, ownership of the church and its possessions was conveyed to the French abbey of Lire, a favoured foundation of the Earl of Leicester, who at that time was Lord of the manor of Wareham.

Medieval Market Town

In 1211, King John granted the burgesses of the town a short-lived civic charter which gave them rights over salmon fishing, grazing, mills, shops, customs duties, mooring fees, weekly markets, an annual fair and their own judicial courts. These rights with their attached monetary perquisites were quickly reclaimed by the crown. A manorial court—the Court Leet—was established. This feudal fossil persisted at Wareham long after such bodies had been abolished elsewhere. Today its activities are limited to overseeing the common land around the town and an annual check of the chimneys, bread and beer at the local hostelries.

However Wareham's fortunes were changing; in 1170, shipping movements were recorded at Poole, which had rapidly developed from a small fishing village to a major port. Its situation, which afforded safe anchorage within the mouth of Poole harbour, was ideal. Ships, which were becoming larger, did not have to wait for the tides to allow them passage up the Frome to Wareham. By 1248, Poole too had received a charter and there is no doubt that its growth precipitated Wareham's decline from a high status Saxon town to a middling medieval market centre.

A number of records survive from this time, giving a tantalising glimpse into the lives of some of the town's inhabitants. Early deeds mention those who bought and sold property and land. Witnesses of these transactions often included the mayor, constables, bailiff and stewards of the town, and these are the first references to these officials.

National policies and politics affected the borough, which was required from 1302 to send two M.P.s to parliament. It was not easy to persuade even the wealthy to take on this high office. Then as now, much time was spent away from home, businesses and families were neglected and great expense was incurred. In the taxations of 1329 and 1332, only 25 people in Wareham paid tax and the town was ranked seventh of the Dorset boroughs. (Poole was ranked eighth.)

In the early Middle Ages, two further parish churches were built. St Peter's at the town crossroads and St Michael's sited off West Street. Chapels-of-Ease were established in North Street (St Nicholas and All Hallows') and South Street (St John the Baptist). There was also a church at Bestwall, but its precise location is unknown. The Black Death, which entered England on the Dorset coast at Melcombe Regis in 1348, had a catastrophic effect not only on the general population, but also on the clergy. The prior of Wareham died together with priests from St Martin's, St Michael's and St Peter's.

Little is known about secular Wareham at this time apart from the founding of an almshouse in 1418, endowed by John Streche for 'six ancient men and five women'. This chantry charity survived the Reformation and to this day Wareham's elderly continue to benefit from Streche's piety and munificence.

Major building work at the priory church in the early 14th century resulted in a large extended chancel with a magnificent east window. A tower was added to the church about 1500 and a porch shortly afterwards. At the same time, a brick-built barn was erected on St John's Hill. This late medieval building survives, albeit elevated and altered over the centuries.

Henry VIII's taxation of 1525 noted Wareham's 75 taxpayers—only the very poor were exempted. It would seem that the town's small community of merchants, shopkeepers, artisans, gentry and peasants lived side by side. The 16th century saw sweeping changes throughout the country, the most dramatic being the dissolution of the monasteries. In 1534, the priory was visited by the king's Commissioners and valued at £4 16s. 8d. It was a small, poor house with fewer than a dozen brothers and had been a cell of the Carthusian priory of Sheen since 1419. In 1535, Wareham's priory was suppressed and its goods and lands sold. The church was acquired for the town; this had far reaching implications for the lesser parish churches which were all to become redundant within the next 150 years.

A number of substantial houses were built during Elizabeth I's reign. On the priory site, a small three-roomed 'hall-house' developed into the complex building which stands there today. The 'Anglebury' in North Street is another house which has seen extension and alteration over the centuries. Standing next to Holy Trinity, numbers 31 and 33 South Street were originally one dwelling. 'Elm House' in North Street is perhaps the most enigmatic structure—its plastered three-storey front disguises 16th-century origins. Next door, 'Long Hall' also dates from this period.

Dissent and Civil War

Radical and often traumatic changes affected all members of society in the 17th century. All males over 16 were required to sign the 'Protestation Returns' in 1642 to confirm their membership of the established church. In all, 300 men from the town's parishes of Lady St Mary, Holy Trinity and St Martin's signed. There appeared to be neither Dissenters nor Catholics in the town but some doubtless signed rather than reveal their religious sympathies.

In the same year the Civil War erupted. Charles I's policies had been almost universally disliked and the town's M.P.'s were among the king's critics. Initially, Wareham sided with the Parliamentarians, but in 1643 the borough was taken by the Royalists. A fierce battle for the town followed, involving 2,000 Cromwellian soldiers and horsemen who trounced the Royalist forces. For the remainder of the war Wareham remained in Parliamentary hands, with a garrison of over 4,000 men billeted in the town. At Stoborough, 100 houses were deliberately razed to aid the Roundheads in their fight for Wareham. However, the promised compensation never materialised.

Sir Anthony Ashley Cooper recommended in 1643 that, because the borough had for a time espoused the Royalist cause, its walls should be destroyed. The town was said to be 'extremely mean-built and its inhabitants almost all dreadful malignants'. Parliament replied that, although the place was 'of no consequence', it could not agree to the destruction. The war had serious implications for Wareham's churches; the incumbents were removed, as most of them inclined towards traditional church doctrine and the Royalist cause. Strict Puritans were installed in their places.

To support the restoration of the monarchy, a new tax was imposed on hearths (fireplaces) between 1662-64. Few were exempted and parish officers were empowered to search properties to determine the number of hearths. There was evasion, apathy, non-payment and false returns on an enormous scale as a response to this unpopular tax. The town had suffered greatly during the Civil War and many properties had been damaged or destroyed. Nevertheless, 139 houses were taxed, most being one, or two, hearth dwellings. Generally properties with three or more fireplaces belonged to prosperous inhabitants—46 of Wareham's houses were in this class.

In 1672, the 'Dissenters' were given permission to build a meeting house. Before this, their services were illegal and their congregations subject to hefty fines if they were discovered. The new church was built at the corner of Wyatts Lane and Church Lane. It would seem that many of the town's inhabitants had broken away from the established church and were worshipping at this new 'Independent Chapel'.

For their part in the Monmouth Uprising, Judge Jeffreys sentenced a number of Dorset men to death at the Dorchester 'Bloody Assizes'. Subsequently, a gallows was set up on West Walls, and five men were hung, drawn and quartered there. (The place is still known as Bloody Banks.) Afterwards their heads were displayed at the crossroads and their quarters on South Bridge.

The Great Fire of Wareham

In 1742 John Hutchins was instituted as Rector of the combined parishes. During his incumbency, he compiled the monumental *History and Antiquities of the County of Dorset*. Subsequent historians owe him a debt of gratitude: Hutchins and Dorset history are synonymous. That same year a small fire destroyed nine houses—fire was a constant hazard where there were timber-built, thatched properties.

Another fire 40 years later almost devastated the town. On Sunday 25 July 1762 at about three o'clock in the afternoon, hot ashes were tipped onto a rubbish heap at the rear of the

Bull's Head Inn on the east side of South Street. A blustery wind blew burning rubbish onto the thatched roof and rapidly set the building alight. This resulted in a conflagration of enormous magnitude. Four hours later, two thirds of the town had been burnt to the ground; 133 buildings were destroyed, including the recently re-built Dissenters' Meeting House. There was no loss of life but damage was estimated at £10,000.

During the next year re-building commenced. Sturdy brick-built houses lined the main streets and the use of thatch was prohibited from the town centre. Buildings and tenements which had previously stood at the cross roads were not replaced. The resulting width of the road in that area is a very attractive feature of modern Wareham. Shortly after the fire, local landowners, the Calcraft estate, bought over half the houses in the town, an important move when voting rights were attached to freeholds. Calcraft properties can be identified today by the metal plaque bearing a four-pointed star which is attached to the brickwork, usually over the front door.

For centuries Wareham's south bridge has carried traffic over the river Frome and into Purbeck. In 1777, the Norman stonework was dismantled and a five-arched, hump-backed bridge was built. This picturesque single-track structure was deemed to be unsuitable for modern traffic and a concrete replacement was erected in 1927.

At the Independent chapel there were problems and disagreements culminating in breakaway congregations who set up new churches at their own expense. In West Street, a chapel was built in 1790 and in South Street a Palladian-style church was consecrated in 1830.

Victorian 'Improvements'

At the close of the century, war with France was imminent and a barracks was built at Westport. In 1814 after the victorious Battle of Trafalgar, a celebration dinner for 960 was held in the town with tables set the length of North and South Streets. Two years later, the short-lived barracks was dismantled.

The first documented school had been established by George Pitt M.P. in 1700. Its teachers were ministers from the parish church. It was not until 1829 that regular schooling became available when a 'British' school was founded by the Nonconformists at their Independent chapel in Church Lane. The following year, a Church of England school was started in the, by now disused, Holy Trinity premises. Both schools moved to larger buildings and eventually amalgamated in 1923. Up until then there had been bitter rivalry between the two establishments.

In 1832, the 'Reform Act' reduced Wareham's two M.P.s to a single member; the town, a 'rotten borough', had only 140 voters. Elections were always volatile occasions, the candidates not averse to bribing and corrupting the electorate. The town was notorious as one of the rowdiest in the country at election time, with fights at meetings commonplace. Wareham was totally disenfranchised in 1885.

Although money had been spent on fittings in the parish church, the fabric of the building had been sorely neglected. In 1840, a decision was taken to demolish the nave; its roof was dangerous, dilapidated and leaked badly, soaking the walls beneath with green slime and mould. In addition, the rector complained about the acoustics and seating, which was damp and inadequate. The chancel and tower were to be retained. Demolition of the nave commenced in May 1841 and two weeks later the 'Celtic' memorial stones were found incorporated as building material in the old church. It was some time before their significance was realised. It became apparent, alas too late, that the nave had been constructed in the early years of the eighth century. In 1842, the church re-opened. Included in the total cost of £2,200 was the new-fangled gas lighting. Throughout the century, the church was altered and modernised, a succession of generous rectors and parishioners leaving memorials in the form of building works and improvements.

In 1847 the railway arrived. The original station at Northport was east of the present building which was completed in 1864. The line linked Wareham with Dorchester, Southampton and London. Due to petty wrangling by the various landowners, it was not until 1885 that the branch line to Swanage was opened. By the end of the century, steam power had a rival—the petrol engine—and motor cars were becoming everyday sights on the town's roads.

A public water supply (from Worgret) was connected in 1906. Controversy had raged since the 1840s. Despite the local doctors' insisting that public health standards depended on clean and plentiful water supplies, the council prevaricated for years before committing themselves and the town ratepayers to what they regarded as a rather frivolous expense.

Wareham Camp

There had been a long tradition of military links with Wareham and the surrounding area; for many years, annual camps had been held for the Territorials and before them, the Militia. When the First World War broke out in 1914, 3,200 men were on exercises at a tented camp on the outskirts of town. The temporary camp became a permanent establishment and grew rapidly on both sides of the Worgret Road, extending beyond the hamlet of Worgret itself. Initially, the military authorities had no time to prepare for large numbers of extra troops and the first arrivals were without uniforms and billeted in the church halls and schools. The soldiers trained all over Purbeck before being sent to France. Up to 7,000 men in the town presented some problems, the most pressing being the lack of public conveniences; five were hurriedly constructed. Wareham Camp was eventually re-located to Bovington in 1922 but, for almost a decade, shopkeepers and particularly publicans had profited from the military presence. Parents of daughters must however have sighed with relief at the camp's departure!

For centuries, Wareham had been a self-sufficient community. Trade Directories list numerous bakers, butchers, drapers, shoemakers etc., as well as the more specialised tradesmen and professional people. Most had premises in the town, often in their own dwelling houses and frequently businesses passed from generation to generation of the same family. Labourers were in great demand on local farms, and numerous women and girls worked as domestic servants. The clay industry also employed many men.

Winston Churchill passes through

In September 1939, a new 'Modern' school opened. Its opening, however, coincided with the outbreak of war. The first children to pass through its doors were evacuees from London who stayed overnight before going on to families in Poole. To prepare for the conflict, senior boys had helped to dig air-raid trenches in the school's extensive grounds to accommodate pupils and staff. The school log-book charted the progress of the war and mirrored the trials and tribulations faced by many at that time.

The school's gym, showers and hall were used by the military on a regular basis. In the summer of 1940, Prime Minister Winston Churchill visited while the school was in use as an 'Advanced Dressing Station'. Although only one bomb fell on Wareham during the war (demolishing cottages next to St Martin's), there were many occasions when the air-raid siren sounded as the town was on the German bombers' flight path to the strategically placed city of Bristol.

The second half of the 20th century has brought many changes. A rapidly increasing population has precipitated development outside the town and in-filling to a high degree within the walls. Despite this, the town centre has retained an air of genteel respectability, the 18th-century properties reflecting its status as a small market town. Through recent difficult economic circumstances, small businesses have continued to provide services for residents and visitors alike. Indeed, tourism is now of vital importance to the local economy.

Just as, two thousand years ago, the area's natural resources determined that Wareham grew and prospered, so it is today. England's largest on-shore oil field operates a few miles from the town, sands and gravels are extracted for an ever expanding construction industry and clay continues to be mined as it has been for centuries. Salmon are still caught in the Frome and, although the weir has long gone, the settlement by it has developed into the town we know today; a borough with a long and sometimes turbulent history eagerly looking forward to the approach and challenges of its third millennium.

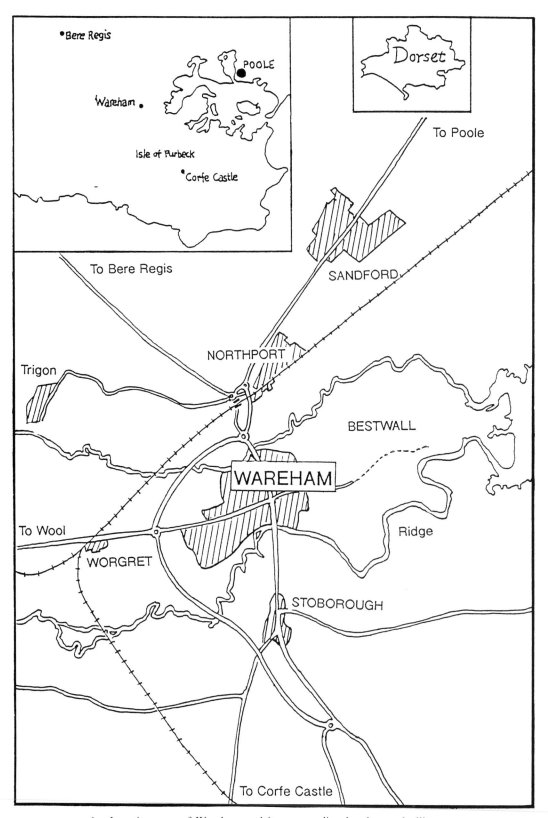

Bere Regis

POOLE

Wareham

Isle of Purbeck

Corfe Castle

Dorset

To Poole

To Bere Regis

SANDFORD

NORTHPORT

Trigon

BESTWALL

WAREHAM

Ridge

To Wool

WORGRET

STOBOROUGH

To Corfe Castle

1. Location map of Wareham and its surrounding hamlets and villages.

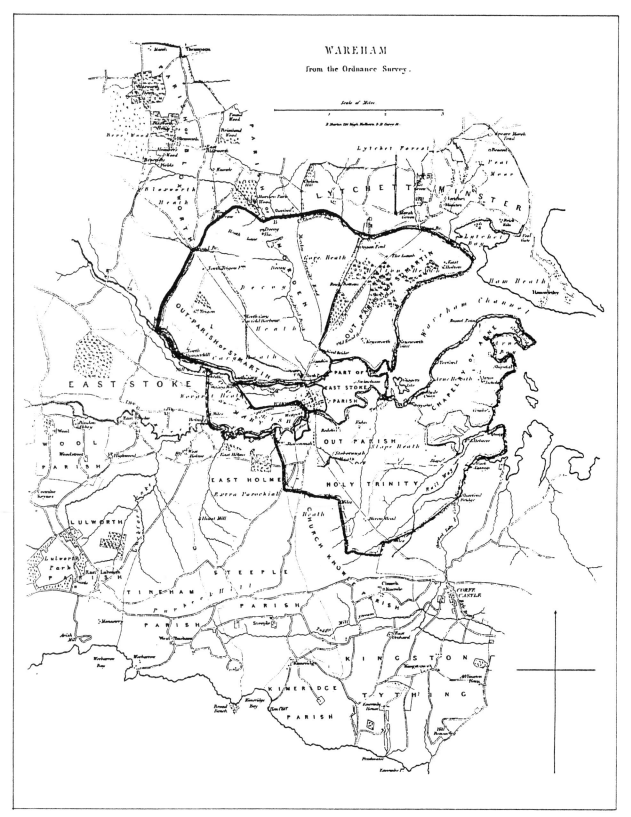

2. Map drawn for the Boundary Commission in 1832 showing the proposed borough extension by the annexation of the Chapelry of Arne. Through this, the town hung on to one M.P. At this time, Bestwall was still part of East Stoke parish and St Martin's was bisected by Morden parish.

3.   Stoborough, *c.*1910. The name means a 'stony hill or barrow' and, indeed, the 'King's Barrow', a Bronze Age burial mound, is sited just outside the village. On the right, small boys play marbles in the road, with no fear of traffic. On the left, the chimneys of Stoborough Elementary school, built in 1871, are visible through the trees.

4.   Stoborough Farm (left), was one of several farms in the village. Behind the farm buildings, there was once a tannery. In 1694, on his death, Francis Stourton, a tanner of Stoborough, left goods and property worth £785, an enormous amount of money for those days.

5. Gay's Stores, *c*.1920. Sydney Gay was the Stoborough baker from before 1915 until after 1939. One of the village's water pumps is outside the shop. Most of the inhabitants of this hamlet were involved in farming or the clay industry but, in 1895, there were, besides the baker, a grocer, a bootmaker, a dressmaker, a wheelwright, and a thatcher.

6. The road to Wareham, 1920. Cows were, and still are, a frequent sight here. The *New Inn* (left), was one of the village's two pubs. Stoborough suffered greatly during the Civil War when most of its houses were demolished to allow the Parliamentary forces to bombard Wareham without impediment.

7. South Causeway, 1910. This raised gravel-topped road had a firm stone base and was the main route out to Purbeck. During wet winters, the road often flooded and flat-bottomed boats were the only way to travel between Wareham and Stoborough. The church of Lady St Mary is visible through the long-since felled trees.

8. William Pike's clay barges being towed by the screw-steamer *Frome*, *c*.1860. The barges carried 400 tons of clay and were crewed by three men. They plied the river until 1941 and were also used to transport coal and corn. The town is idyllically depicted here but, despite this, the major buildings can be identified.

9. A low aerial photograph taken from Bestwall, looking up the Frome, *c*.1930. The recently built concrete bridge is visible centre left. Redcliffe Yacht Club was formed about this time by Percy Westerman, who lived on a houseboat on the river for many years. He was a prolific and popular author of over 170 adventure books for boys.

10. (*Above left*) View up the Frome, 1900. On the left, the well worn tow path leads to Redcliffe and Ridge. The 'Priory' is dwarfed by the church, which has been a landmark to generations of sailors navigating the Frome. On the riverbank is Wareham Boating Club with its own slipway. The boathouse was re-built opposite Abbot's Quay after the First World War.

11. (*Above*) Yachts at Redcliffe, *c*.1920. Redcliffe Farm (right) was built in the 17th century, drastically altered in the 19th and demolished in the 20th century. Roman potters were active in this area and evidence of their activities can still be found in local ditches and mole hills. 'Redcliffe' is the red sandstone outcrop which gives its name to the place.

12. (*Left*) In 1791, Josiah Wedgwood contracted the Pike Brothers to supply china clay. A railway was constructed in 1860 to carry clay from their Furzebrook works to Ridge wharf. The engine Tertius was purchased in 1886 and is shown on 11 May 1911 transporting visitors from the English Ceramic Society. Today the company operates as English China Clays Ltd.

13.   Built in 1894, the paddle steamer *Totnes Castle* had plied the river Dart. She was sold in August 1912 and re-named the *Wareham Queen*. Until 1923 she was used for pleasure trips on the Frome and around Poole Harbour. On the left is the tow path, a popular walking place today for residents and visitors alike.

14.   South Bridge, 1910. In 1788, the Norman bridge was rebuilt; its replacement incorporated some of the medieval stonework. This five-arched single-tracked structure proved too narrow for modern traffic and was demolished in 1927. The bottom of South Street was subsequently widened and Bridge House on the Quay was drastically reduced in size.

15. Steam crane working on the new bridge, 1927. After the Great War, motor traffic increased dramatically. In 1919, the Borough Engineer attended a county conference on highways, and suggested that both the north and south bridges needed widening. In 1927, the old Purbeck stone bridge was dismantled and replaced by the present unimaginative concrete structure.

16.   The remains of a sword, the most prestigious of all Anglo-Saxon weapons, was found in the river gravels during the rebuilding of South Bridge in 1927. It survived almost intact. The iron blade was corroded and upon the horn grip were remnants of an ownership formula. The 10th-century sword was deposited in the County Museum.

17.   South Bridge, 1914. In the Middle Ages, the quay east of the bridge was the responsibility of the townsmen who had to keep it clean and well maintained. The mayor received the benefit of tolls levied on users of this quay. Abbot's Quay, west of the bridge, belonged to the Abbots of Sherborne who held Holy Trinity church.

18. The Quay, 1910. The town's gutters were flushed by the horse-drawn water barrel which held 20 gallons of water. Middle right, the *Rising Sun* was a pub from 1810-1931. Next door was coal merchant Philip Gillingham's premises; his family had been Wareham tradesmen for over a century. The stucco-fronted warehouse (left) was originally a dwelling house.

19. East side of the Quay, 1901. In the 1840s the Quay was repaired after years of neglect; all the properties there had been destroyed in the 1762 fire. Oakley Brothers of Poole operated a granary and warehouse (1859-92) adjoining P.P. Gillingham's premises. On the riverbank, Henry Cox, fishmonger of West Street, hired out row boats.

20. The Old Granary Tea Rooms, 1935. This popular eating house was run by the Misses Sydenham and Miss Carter in premises which had been converted from Gillingham's warehouse. In 1948, advertisements stated 'ample parking on the Quay and open on Sundays'. The boathouse next to the Granary belonged to James Habgood who hired out rowing boats.

21. On 23 July 1911, Captain Charles Radclyffe foul-hooked a 203lb. sturgeon at Bindon Mill on the Frome. It had been observed in the river for many weeks beforehand. The fish, 9ft.3ins. in length, is the largest and heaviest to have been taken in an English river and the only known sturgeon to have been caught on rod and line in England.

22. Captain (later, Major) Radclyffe presented the fish to King George V, who requested that it might be displayed in the County Museum at Dorchester. The fish, common in south Russian rivers, is a rare visitor to English waters. The captain's Daimler with fish strapped to the top is parked on the Quay with Gillingham's coal warehouse in the background.

23. Mr. Henry Thorne (1856-1946) painted by H.J.S. Clarke. In his obituary Thorne was called 'The Grand Old Man of the Frome' and, like generations of his family before him, he was a fisherman and netsman. A life-long ambition to net a big salmon was fulfilled when he was 78 years old and landed a monster 45-pounder.

24.   Until the early 1900s, regattas were held each summer on the Frome. Large crowds gathered on the south bank of the river to watch, many viewing from their own or hired, decorated dinghies. Events, which were always held at high tide, included swimming, diving and competitions on a greasy pole.

25. Fire engine on the Quay, *c.*1910. The Voluntary Fire Brigade consisted of a superintendent and 10 men. Their brass helmets had been purchased by the council in 1885 for 1s. 6d. each. When a fire broke out, the firemen were alerted by the Almshouse bell. At the time of the Great Fire in 1762, the town had two primitive fire engines.

26. The old fire engine was replaced in 1916 when an appliance was purchased from Lord Shaftesbury at Cranborne. It seated a driver and six men comfortably and could be pulled by four or six horses. During the First World War, the military borrowed the engine regularly for fire practice.

27. The 'Muddlecombe Men', 1933. The group developed from the Court Leet proceedings and became involved in charity work all over the south. They regularly hired the fire engine and, while they attended local carnivals, the town was without any fire cover! The *New Inn* on the Quay was their headquarters and landlord Gordon Sansom directed Muddlecombe antics for many years.

28. Officers of the Court Leet at the *New Inn*. Wareham's Court Leet is a relic of the medieval manor court. Its officers, a steward, bailiff, and hayward, two constables, two aletasters, two bread weighers, two scavengers, two chimney peepers and a leather sealer have an annual inspection of local hostelries and are still responsible for the town common.

29. Beating the bounds. This ancient annual custom evolved before written records were kept, when parish officials and clergy perambulated the boundaries. The beating of the 'Admiralty Jurisdiction water bounds' between Wareham and Poole was revived in 1921. The boat with civic party left Wareham Quay to rendezvous with their Poole counterparts at Redcliffe Atwell in Poole Harbour.

30.   The winter of 1963 paralysed Dorset. Severe weather started in January and lasted for six weeks. Mr. Monty Best, whose family have traded in the town for generations, regards the almost-frozen river Frome.

31. The Priory, 1900. At that time the home of Mrs. Annie Beale who let apartments there. Previously it had belonged to the Phippards, solicitors in the town. The house, parts of which date to the 16th century, stands on the site of the Norman Priory. It is also reputed to be the site of the Saxon nunnery.

32. John Hutchins was born in 1698 and was rector of Wareham from 1742-73. He spent much of his life researching for the county history which was published in 1774, a year after his death. *The History and Antiquities of the County of Dorset* is now in its third edition.

33. This watercolour from 1864 was based on earlier sketches drawn before the 1842 rebuilding. The church had been re-paved in 1745, re-glazed in 1751 and galleries and box pews installed in 1761. The Saxon windows and aisle arches are intact, as is the Norman chancel arch with Georgian coat of arms above.

34. Lady St Mary, founded *c*.700, and illustrated in this mid-18th-century print, was one of the first stone-built churches in Dorset. The nave displays the original window openings, while the aisle windows range in date from the 13th-15th centuries. The defaced and weathered crucifixion over the doorway is now in the north aisle of the church.

35. Lady St Mary from Church Green. The four-stage crenellated tower dates to 1500 and the porch was added shortly afterwards. During the drastic rebuilding of 1842, the tower and porch were left unaltered and intact. In 1882, new stained glass was acquired for the west window. The tower has a peal of 10 bells.

36. Lady St Mary from the east. The splendid chancel with its magnificent window were constructed in 1325. The work was probably instigated and paid for by the French mother house at Lire. On the left are the outbuildings of the 'Priory' and, in the foreground, the 1880 extension to the churchyard, which was enlarged four times between 1826-1914.

37. Lady St Mary interior (1890s). Rector from 1881-88, the Rev. Pelham Stokes began a radical programme of improvements, the cost of which was mostly borne by himself. The western gallery 'considered unsightly' was removed, the church re-paved, re-seated and a new heating and lighting system installed. The north and south galleries, however, were retained.

38. Lady St Mary interior (1903). Canon Selwyn Blackett served the church and town for 48 years and during his incumbency the improvements, including the removal of the remaining galleries, continued. The celebrated London firm of Clayton and Bell installed stained glass in the east window between 1886-90; the lights were paid for by the town's wealthier citizens.

39. Lead fonts are rare—there are only 31 in the country. This one is unique, being hexagonal and cast whole. It is decorated with images of the 12 apostles. In 1150 the church was granted to the Norman abbey of Lire and the font dates from this period. The octagonal Purbeck marble base is 13th century.

40. The War Memorial in Lady St Mary churchyard was erected to commemorate those servicemen buried during the First World War. The small, rectangular gravestones mark military graves and belong to Canadians, Australians, Englishmen and Germans. A sad and salutary reminder of the futility of conflict. The cottages in the background were known as 'Davis Row'.

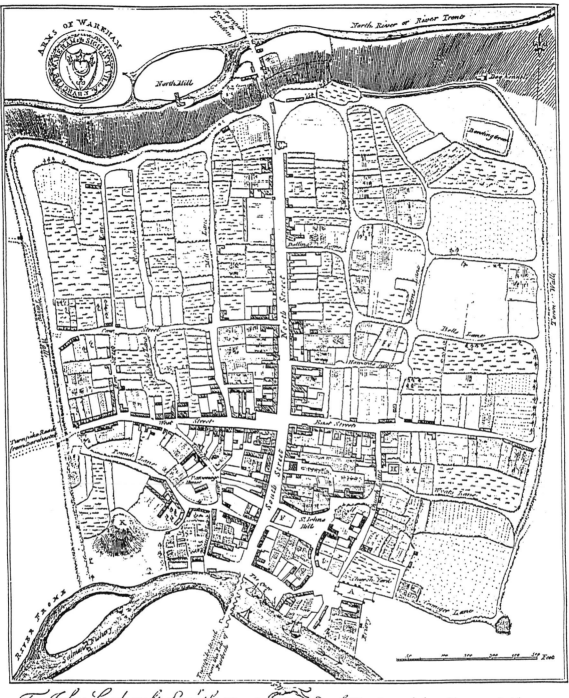

To John Calcraft Esq.ʳ this Plan of Wareham, is humbly inscribed by

The Author:

A. S.ᵗ Mary's Church.
B. Trinity Church.
C. S.ᵗ Martin's Church.
D. Town Hall formerly S.ᵗ Peter's Church.
E. Formerly S.ᵗ Michael's Church.

F. Formerly S.ᵗ John's Church.
G. Formerly Allhallows Chapel.
H. Dissenter's Meeting House.
I. Alms House.
K. Formerly the Castle.

41. This map was drawn by John Hutchins for his 'History'. Most of the houses are clustered in the south of the town and along the main streets. The positions of the major buildings are indicated. The north part of the town was mostly gardens and allotments and remained so until this century, when every available plot of land has been developed.

42. The south approach to Wareham as depicted in a print of *c*.1815. Holy Trinity (left) was the town's major parish church until the Reformation. On the Quay, Bridge House and the Granary are recognisable and far right is Lady St Mary. Boats, such as the lighters shown, transported goods to and from Poole.

43. Bottom of South Street, *c*.1900. On the left, Stephen Bennett's brewery; he lived opposite at Bridge House. The family had owned the business since the late 1700s. The brewery warehouse is covered in adverts—photographer James Bridle was the billposter. Behind, Holy Trinity church was then in use as a parish meeting room.

44.   View up South Street, 1860. Bridge House is on the right, its frontage protected by ornamental bollards. The houses in this part of South Street were demolished for road widening in 1926-7. Opposite is Holy Trinity, which was used as the National School from 1830-85. The street is dominated by the cupola of the old town hall (centre).

45.   View down South Street, *c*.1900. This photograph was produced for Miss Hannah Kelsey who had a stationer's-cum-toy shop on the right. She was the town's first telephonist. Best's the fruiterers have been trading there since the late 1930s. The road, which curves away to South Bridge, was widened when the bridge was rebuilt in 1927.

46. South Street, *c.*1910. The old Police Station on the right was built in 1859 when the County Constabulary was formed. A similar design was used for Police Stations all over Dorset. Thomas Eeles was the first superintendent. By 1915, Henry Toop oversaw two sergeants and 15 constables.

47. The *Black Bear Hotel*, first mentioned in 1722, was destroyed in 1762 and re-built as an elegant inn. The porch, a later addition, protected travellers while they waited for their coaches. The 'Emerald' stage coach departed from the *Bear* to London six days a week. By 1900, the hotel advertised good accommodation for motorists, cyclists and yachtsmen.

48. The original effigy of a black bear no doubt represented bear baiting, which was popular and legal until the mid-19th century. Itinerants with their dancing bears also provided amusement for the unsophisticated masses. Local legend states, 'if the bear falls from the porch, the world will end'. To prevent this, he is securely chained down.

49. The 'Manor House' was built in 1712 for Mr. George Gould. It survived the fire and is Wareham's only Grade 1 listed building. The front is faced with ashlared blocks of Purbeck stone, the back and sides are brick. The house itself has seen little alteration but in 1978 a shopping precinct was developed in its once extensive garden.

50. Joseph Seller Burr, 18 South Street in 1890. He sold 'high class groceries at moderate prices' as well as wines, spirits, ales and stout. Like most shopkeepers he worked long hours—from 6 a.m. to 10 p.m. was not unusual. After 9 p.m. on Saturdays there were many bargains, as all perishables had to be sold.

51. Worlds Stores traded next door to Burr's from 1915-20, then took over Burr's premises. The old shop was extended and the frontage altered. The original door and windows to the left were modernised and a new shop sign installed. Maximum use was still made of the window space. The shop moved to 3 North Street in the early 1960s.

52. The *Castle Inn*, 21 South Street, *c.*1930 was the *White Hart* from 1806-72. It was then refurbished, renamed and advertised as 'an old established market house with luncheons, teas and accommodation'. In 1895, the firemen repaired to the *Castle* after extinguishing a nearby fire. The engine was left unlit and unattended causing a passer-by a nasty leg injury!

53. Sansom, Speed and Co., 10 South Street, c.1910. Their large premises displayed furniture and ironmongery inside and outside the shop. Established as Selby's before 1790, the business was one of the oldest in Wareham. Albert Speed had moved on to West Street by 1915 but Sansom's traded there until the 1970s.

54. The top of South Street, late 1950s. James Foot's corn and seed merchant's shop was demolished in 1978. For nearly 100 years the same business had been conducted from the premises. In 1885, Cann and Son were corn dealers, seedsmen, coal, coke and salt merchants as well as hauliers and agents for the London and South Western Railway Company.

55. Unitarian Chapel, South Street, was built in 1830 to seat 250. The Palladian-style building served a break-away group which had split from the Congregational community in Church Lane in 1828, due to doctrinal differences. The church closed in the late 1960s and the premises were converted for use by the Conservative Club.

56. To celebrate Queen Victoria's Golden Jubilee in 1887, the town was profusely decorated, with tradesmen and householders all competing to outdo each other. Church services in the morning were followed by a free dinner for 800. In the afternoon, the be-medalled Sunday school children assembled on St John's Hill to parade through the town and thence to Bestwall for games.

57.   The barn on St John's Hill was built *c*.1500 and is the oldest of its type in Dorset. The central doorway is original, the rest of the building has been altered and modified over the years. During the 18th century it was a malthouse and later a forge where the Newberys who were blacksmiths traded from the early 1880s until after the Second World War.

58.   Crossroads, late 1840s. All the buildings here were newly built after the fire. On the right is the Town Hall, in front of which is the 'town pump'—the only source of water for many. Opposite, the *Red Lion*, a posting inn, was established in the late 1600s. Neighbouring houses belonged to the town's élite.

59. Built in 1768 and photographed in 1860, the Georgian Town Hall replaced the medieval church of St Peter which had been converted into a municipal building in the 1600s. The new premises provided an upper-floor Town Hall, and a ground-floor Corn Exchange, schoolroom and jail. Correct time was ensured by both a clock and a sun dial.

60. Montague Guest of Canford, Wareham's last M.P. For the 1886 election, the town was amalgamated with Poole. During a political rally at the Corn Exchange, fights constantly broke out, maintaining Wareham's reputation as 'the rowdiest place in the county at election time'. Guest, a Conservative, was the victor.

61.   Town Hall and Marshallsay's, 1911. The Corn Exchange was in great demand for private functions. Opposite was Marshallsay's Central Supply Stores, which sold wines, spirits and high class groceries. The business opened in the 1860s and flourished for 70 years. The building is decorated with flags and bunting to celebrate the coronation of George V.

62.   The new Town Hall was opened in 1870 by Cornelius Yearsley, mayor and landlord of the *Red Lion*. The architect was Crickmay who had designed St Martin's House four years earlier. Charles Cox, fishmonger, game and poultry supplier, took over the shop (extreme left) from his father Henry in 1911. The business had been established in West Street in the early 1880s.

63. A civic ceremony followed a thanksgiving service at the parish church to celebrate the coronation of George V on 22 July 1911. On a raised platform in front of the Corn Exchange, the mayor read out a loyal address to the new king. Festivities had begun at 5.30 a.m. but were halted later in the afternoon by heavy rain.

64. In the late 19th century, the *Red Lion* was the town's premier hotel, managed by Cornelius Yearsley, several times mayor. It was noted for its sumptuous seven-course meals, the meat from Dugdale's and the vegetables from its own farm and gardens. The 1920s vehicles are parked on the hotel forecourt.

65.   The anticipated arrival on 4 August 1914 of 3,200 Territorial Reserves at the camp site on the town outskirts was cancelled at short notice. Northover's, the Worgret bakers, had been asked to provide bread for the troops and they were left with 1,000 loaves which were given away outside the Town Hall. The Town Crier broadcast the free offer.

66.   Between September and November 1914, up to 7,000 men were stationed at the tented camp on the Worgret Road. They slept 22 to a bell tent, all with feet to the centre pole. That autumn the rain was torrential and prolonged and the camp became a quagmire. It was not until November that the building of wooden huts commenced.

67.   Huts and tents, 1914. The contract for building a permanent camp was won by Macdonald Gibbs, supervising engineers to the War Department. For a time, until the permanent accommodation was erected, tents and huts were sited side by side. This group of soldiers had responsibilities for mounted transport; they all hold horse whips.

68. The West Yorks Transport in 1915, with their requisitioned horses and mules, many of which had been purchased from local farmers and tradesmen. The road had recently been laid but not yet rolled. At the stores (left) the storemen frequently had to be bribed to issue the correct fitting uniform.

69. By 1917, Wareham Camp was considered to be the finest in England. The huts, 60ft. by 30ft., slept 30 men and were ranged on the north side of Worgret Road. Better accommodation was provided for the officers on the south side of the road. The gravelled tracks between the huts were known as lines. This card dates from 1915.

70. Troops marching down West Street, 1915. There were constant movements of troops in and out of the camp. During May, a whole battalion marched out of town on its journey to the front. One poignant postcard message reads, 'Dear mother, we are moving from here to Winchester, we are having to march there'.

71. The local press reported in February 1915 that a 'Cyclists Company of the Division had been formed'. The 280 officers and men were selected from the various regiments. Some of these were deployed on coastguard duty along the Purbeck coast. The *Antelope* on the left, together with the town's ten other pubs, did a roaring trade at this time.

72. The funeral of sergeant Charles Stevens of the 10th West Yorks regiment, 17 March 1915. The body was conveyed by six fellow sergeants and the cortège was followed by a company of the deceased's regiment. Bands of the 10th West Yorks and the 6th Dorsets accompanied the procession, and a firing party discharged volleys over the grave.

73. The sight of troops marching through the town was commonplace. They regularly marched to and from exercises and military bands marched to various venues in the town to entertain the citizens. Ingrouille's (right) continued a long tradition of dispensing drugs and medicines from this shop. It has been a chemist's since before 1840.

74. By October 1914, the Y.M.C.A. operated from a large marquee at the camp. This provided much needed leisure facilities for the troops. At the beginning of December, a 30ft. by 100ft. permanent building was opened by the Dowager Lady Wimborne. Next door, the Garrison Cinema, dubbed 'the Gaff' by the soldiers, doubled as a church on Sundays.

75.　Photographed in 1906, the Union Workhouse on the western outskirts of the town was opened in 1837. There was a uniform for men, women and children which was supplied by local outfitters. In this grim building, husbands, wives and children were separated, their only crimes being poverty or infirmity. In the 1940s, it became a geriatric hospital known as 'Christmas Close'.

76.　West Walls, 1924. Earthen ramparts, constructed about A.D. 876, as part of King Alfred's defence policy to repel the Vikings, surround the town on three sides. Of the original fortified places in Saxon Wessex, only the defences of Wareham and Wallingford survive almost intact. Wareham's walls escaped destruction in 1646 when parliament considered their 'Slighting'. Corfe Castle was not so fortunate!

77. Between 1952-4, excavations were conducted on West Walls. The findings stated that ninth-century defences overlay Iron Age and Roman levels. Sands and gravels from an outer ditch were used to construct the earthwork which was strengthened with through-timbers. The ditch was 50ft. wide and the height of the rampart from the ditch base was 26ft.

78. Cock Pits, West Walls. Victorian antiquaries mistakenly considered this area to be a Roman amphitheatre. The name 'Cockpits' must have been acquired when cock fighting was a legal sport and was held there. In the early 1900s, the choir and clergy of Lady St Mary led communal hymn singing there, the outdoor congregation sitting on the sloping walls.

79.   Houses at Westport, *c*.1900. The early 19th-century cottages at Westport were erected directly on top of the Saxon defences, as was the Victorian villa 'Belle Vue', which was built in 1885. Even after 10 centuries, the depth of the ditch was still considerable.

80.   Almshouse allotments, Westport, 1908. Two allotment holders (centre) are no doubt discussing horticultural matters. Behind, the construction of the new Streche Almshouses begins. Local builder, Albert Marsh, whose company still trades today, did the building work.

81. The Town Band, 1908, posing outside the half-completed Almshouses, hats borrowed from a cavalry regiment who were camped nearby. The band had been established for at least half a century when, in 1898, the town council took over responsibility. The band practised in the Town Hall and regularly played in the town and outlying districts.

82. Almshouses at Westport, 1910. The outmoded East Street buildings were replaced by this 'Tudor style' range in 1908. Rooms were provided for 11 pensioners who received 11s. weekly besides new clothes, beef and best coals at Christmas. The railings were removed during the Second World War and the saplings are now 60ft. high.

83. The relaxed football team of 1895-6. They had recently won the Dorset Junior Cup and the extreme youth of the side is apparent. The captain, seated left, wears the badge of Wareham Football Club. The team was disbanded in 1914 and was reformed after a public meeting in 1919.

84. East Street, *c.*1900. The *Three Tuns*, on the left, opened in 1768 and closed in 1906. The *Duke of Wellington*, next door, opened *c.*1821 and is still trading. In 1890, the town had eight public water pumps, two of which were in East Street. For the majority, water still had to be fetched and stored in earthenware jars.

85. Almshouses, East Street, 1915. Endowed by John Streche in 1418, the Almshouses were rebuilt in 1741 by Henry Drax and John Pitt, the town's M.Ps. Rooms were provided for 'six ancient men and five women'. At one time only members of the established church were considered eligible for charity vacancies. The building was let out as tenements in 1908.

86.   East Street, with the old Almshouses on the left, *c*.1915. The steam roller (centre left) was hired when the roads were re-gravelled. In 1914, North Street and Worgret Road were so worn by the military that granite was used for repairs. On the right is William Churchill's 'Good Luck' photographic studio. He was in business from *c*.1895-1923.

87.   View up East Street, *c*.1920. On the left is Bennett Bros., bakers and grocers. The business was established by Jonathan Bennett in the mid-1850s, he also had a confectionery shop in North Street. During 1917, Bennetts advised their customers to consider drinking more coffee and cocoa due to the desperate war-time shortages of tea.

88.   Bestwall Villas, East Street, 1900. A spate of house building in the late 19th century provided modern accommodation for the more prosperous. Bestwall Villas were built in the late 1880s and contrast dramatically with the old cottages opposite which were typical of the houses available for the working classes.

89.   Far end of East Street, 1900. Gravel roads with stone-lined gutters were a feature of the town at this time. On the right, the 17th- and 19th-century cottages were demolished in the 1960s. The gate leads to Bestwall (a corruption of by-the-east-wall), where the land had been part of East Stoke parish until 1888.

90.   North Bestwall Farm, *c.*1900. There were three farms on the Bestwall peninsula; North and South Bestwall and Swineham. In 1900, the tenant of North Bestwall complained to the council that horses grazing on the nearby walls were damaging the farm's thatched buildings. The track in front of the house leads directly to the shores of Poole Harbour.

91.   On 8 August 1912, during exercises of the Territorials in Purbeck, one of the two Royal Aero Corps aircraft landed at Bestwall at 6.30 a.m. and remained there until early evening. The pilot, Major Webb, had landed at the invitation of the mayor. A large crowd gathered to view this highly unusual and exciting event.

AEROPLANE AT WAREHAM.
"AUGUST 8 1912"

92. Old Meeting House, later known as the Independent chapel, Church Lane, *c*.1830. By the early 18th century, Wareham had a large number of influential 'dissenters' who worshipped at these Church Lane premises. The Nonconformists built their first church in 1672 but it was not until 1824 that they acquired their own burial ground.

93. Independent (later Congregational) chapel, 1890. Destroyed in the Great Fire, the church was rebuilt on the old foundations at a cost of £500. During renovations in 1872, charred wood, molten lead and burnt brick were evidence of the ferocity of the 1762 conflagration. North and south wings were added in 1860 and 1895. The British School met there from 1829-50.

94.   Cottages, Church Lane, *c*.1900. This house was built soon after 1770 and the stable conversion and bay window date from the 19th century. All but two of the buildings in this street were destroyed in the 'Fire of Wareham'. An Act of Parliament subsequently forbade the storage of fuel or the use of thatch as roofing in this area.

95.   The bottom of West Street was known as Market Place. In 1895, Randall's (right) had recently moved from North Street. Opposite, George Dicker had opened his second shop which only dealt in groceries. Next door to him, Mary Cleall, 'plumber, painter and cycle agent', carried on her late husband's business.

96.   George Dicker (third right) initially traded in West Street as a grocer and provision merchant in the early 1880s. By 1895, his speciality ham and bacon business was conducted from West Street, and the grocery shop from Market Place. Dickers were noted for their famous sausages and the recipe died with old George.

97.   A rare view of West Street and St Michael's Lane, *c*.1900. On the left, an early Georgian town house with its Victorian bay window. The two adults chat outside the British School; opposite is Mrs. Charlotte Clark's residence, built in the 1870s. Her son and grandson were to become eminent and respected solicitors in the town.

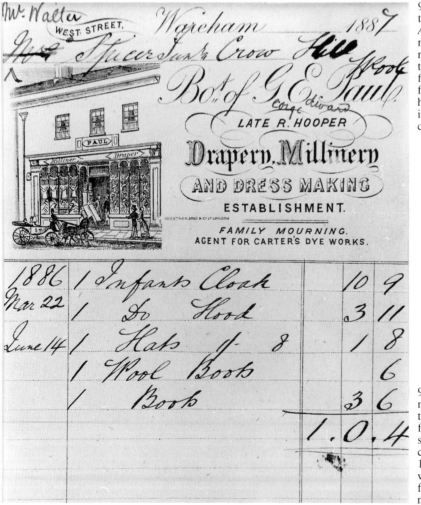

Mr. Walter
WEST STREET.
Wareham 1887

Bot. of George Edward Paul

LATE R. HOOPER

Drapery, Millinery
AND DRESS MAKING
ESTABLISHMENT.

FAMILY MOURNING.
AGENT FOR CARTER'S DYE WORKS.

1886	1 Infants Cloak		10	9
Mar 22	1 Do Hook		3	11
June 14	1 Hats 1/- 8		1	8
	1 Wool Boots			6
	1 Book		3	6
			1.0.4	

98.   Established in Wareham in 1854, the Oddfellows first met at the *Antelope*. Their large, affluent membership enabled them to build a new hall in West Street in 1889. During the First World War it hosted clubs for non-commissioned officers, and frequent military band concerts were held there. For the last seventy years it has been the home of the town's cinema.

99.   George Paul, a draper and milliner, traded in West Street from the early 1880s to 1931. An advert from 1900 notes that the shop also sold household linens, knitting wools, carpets and linos. The billhead from 1887 shows the shop front as it was when Paul had taken over the premises from Robert Hooper, a draper and silk merchant.

100. By 1823, Edward Davis had a butcher's shop at 19 West Street. Joseph Rose took over this established business in 1903. Animals were kept alive on the premises and slaughtered when needed to ensure fresh meat. At Christmas, beasts were paraded through the streets so that customers could view their prospective festive joints! Basil Curtis took over the business in 1951.

101. Joseph Rose promised 'express delivery to all parts of the district daily'. He advertised that families would be supplied with the finest quality meat at the lowest prices. At a time when most shops delivered by bicycle or horse and cart, great status was attached to motorised delivery vehicles.

102.   Cleeve Bros, *c*.1950. Alfred Cleeve opened as a wheelwright at 8 West Street in 1898 and quickly expanded to coach, van and waggon building. By 1915, 'Cleeve Bros.' were advertised as 'motor engineers, garage and cars for hire'. The first petrol licences had been issued to Randall's the chemist and Drew's the ironmongers in 1895.

103.   Wellsteads, 41 West Street, *c*.1925. Trade directories list Fred Wellstead as a draper but in addition he was also a general dealer selling such diverse items as soap powder, cigarettes and confectionery. The building is early 19th-century with an original bow window and front door.

104. The civic procession to celebrate the coronation of Edward VII in 1902 included the mayor and corporation as well as the town's clergy. They marched up West Street to the Recreation Ground where amusements had been laid on. Tom Wellstead's shop at the top of West Street is suitably decorated.

105.   Top of West Street, *c.*1910. The bow window of Tom Wellstead's shop had been replaced with a larger expanse of glass. The cottages on West Walls were demolished in 1924 and replaced with modern dwellings. A tollhouse had originally stood foreground right, a tollkeeper would have collected fees from users of the turnpike road to Dorchester until the mid-1800s.

106.   Tom Wellstead outside his furniture shop at the top of West Street, *c.*1914. Furniture was delivered by the horse-drawn waggons. The shop was run by the family from 1878-1973. In 1915 there were three other Wellsteads in business in the town; George, a china and glass dealer, George junior, a shopkeeper and Frank, a draper.

107. Market Place, *c.*1950. Due to increased traffic through the town, traffic lights were installed at the crossroads. Up the road, at the Oddfellows Hall, the 'Rex' was (and still is) a thriving cinema. Many of the Victorian and Edwardian shop fronts were still intact but the age of plate glass was soon to make its presence felt.

108. Aerial view of the town, looking north east, taken in the 1950s. The wide main streets divide the town into four quarters. In the south west, 'Castle Close' overlooks the Frome, its medieval inner and outer baileys are still traceable in the curves of Pound Lane, Trinity Lane and West Street.

109.   The modern house 'Castle Close' was built in 1911 for Edward Seymer Clark, a local solicitor. The house sits on part of the 70ft. square keep of the Norman fortress. Domesday Book records that after the Norman Conquest 130 houses were destroyed in the town, many of them no doubt razed to facilitate building the castle.

110. In 1950, Mr. Harry Clark excavated and revealed substantial foundations of Wareham Castle 15ft. below the present ground surface. The outer wall of the keep survived to a height of 12ft. and consisted of alternate courses of brown heathstone and Purbeck limestone. Pottery from the site was a mixture of local and continental wares dating from 11th-13th centuries.

111. Pound Lane, c.1900. The cottage on the left had recently had its thatched roof replaced with tiles. On the right is the gate of the town pound; for centuries all strays were impounded there and only released upon the payment of a fine to the Lord of the Manor. The tower of Lady St Mary is visible in the distance.

112. Panton's Brewery staff (a woman caretaker, foreman, 17 men and 3 lads), *c*.1890. There was a brewery in Pound Lane by 1720. The next century, Pantons were brewing there and they also had breweries in Swanage and Ringwood. When James Panton died in 1897, the business was purchased by Strongs of Romsey who closed the Wareham brewery in 1900.

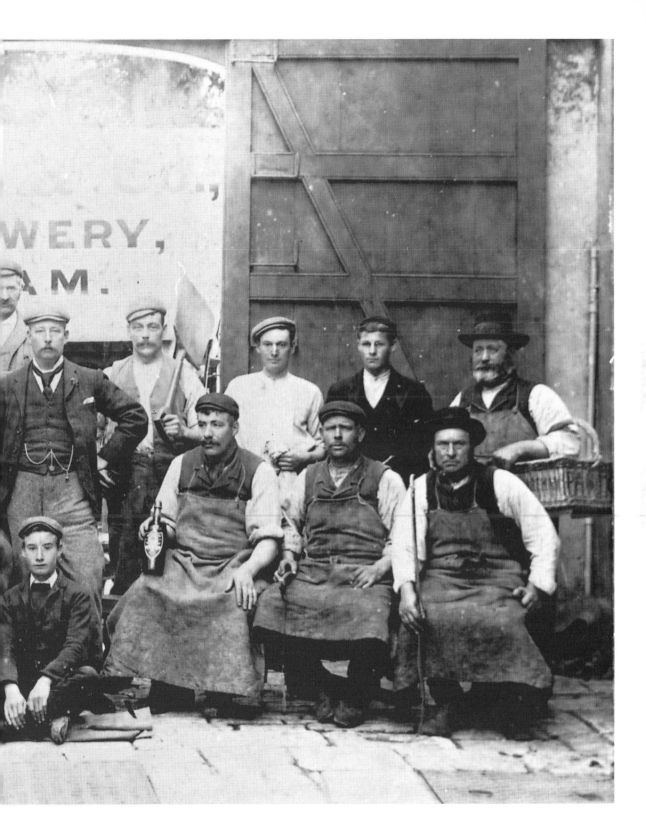

113. Charles Lander Elmes (1845-1928) and his wife Ann, née Wills (1844-1915) were a typical Wareham family. Charles worked for Panton's the brewers and, before him, his father had been a shoemaker. Ann's family were clay cutters from Stoborough. The photograph was taken by William Churchill at his 'Good Luck' studio in East Street, *c.*1895.

114. West Walls and Cow Lane, *c*.1910. The thatched cottages were demolished and replaced by modern houses in 1930. In the distance on West Walls is 'Bloody Banks'. In 1213 this was the site of the hanging of Peter de Pomfret and in 1685 the execution place of five Dorset rebels sentenced to death by Judge Jeffreys after the Monmouth Uprising.

115. Cow Lane, *c*.1900. This narrow lane, typical of the back streets of Wareham, had probably been a droveway to the Town Walls and common for sheep and cattle kept in the town. The picturesque cottages on the left were eventually replaced by houses similar to those opposite which had been built in the late 1890s.

116. Myrtle Cottage, Cow Lane, *c*.1900. On 4 June 1895, a letter from the Inspector of Factories stated that the premises were being used as a dressmaker's shop and that the workroom appeared to be overcrowded. The Misses Diffey, the owners, promised to rectify matters immediately. Trade Directories of 1895 note three other dressmakers in the town.

117. Mount Pleasant, North Walls, *c*.1920. In 1895, the cottages on the right were described as 'unfit for human habitation with their roofs and ceilings in a dilapidated state'. The owners were urged to instigate repairs as soon as possible. At the bottom of the steep lane was the *Lord Nelson* pub, opened shortly after the battle of Trafalgar in 1815.

118.   Foundation stone laying at Bell's Orchard Council Estate, 1920. In 1918, under Central Government initiative, a Housing Committee was set up to look into housing needs after the War. There was a desperate shortage of suitable accommodation for the working classes in the town. William Fookes, the Borough Surveyor, was appointed architect of the scheme.

119.   St Martin's and the top of North Street, 1895. The fact that the church was redundant during the 19th century probably saved it from a 'Victorian Restoration'. Cattle and sheep were a familiar sight on the town's roads as they were brought in to the weekly market and farmers living in town regularly moved their beasts onto the common.

120.   St Martin's, *c.*1900, before its restoration. The east window is bricked in and ivy clambers up the south side of the building. The Saxon style 'long and short' work is visible where the nave and north aisle join. The path is known as 'Lady's Walk', a quiet place for the town's gossips to catch up on the latest news.

121. Queen Victoria's Diamond Jubilee, 19 June 1897. A newspaper report stated 'the old church of St. Martin's which has not been used for divine service for 200 years, has been renovated making it fit for worship. The rector officiated to a packed congregation, with old style music using violins, piccolos etc. Sixteen infants were baptised including some named Victoria or Martin'.

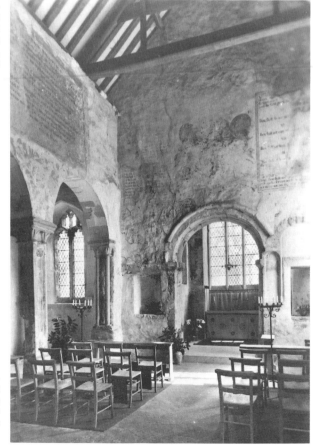

122. On 3 November 1936, the tiny church was re-dedicated. During restoration work, traces of wall paintings dating from 12th-19th centuries were discovered and conserved. The chancel and north aisle arches are rounded and typically Norman. An original small and narrow Saxon-style window survives in the north wall of the chancel.

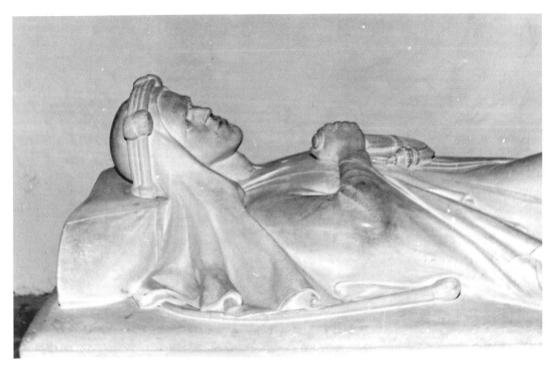

123. T.E. Lawrence (1888-1935) died following a motor cycle accident at Bovington. In 1936, Eric Kennington was commissioned by the Lawrence family to design a suitable memorial. A figure, clad in Arab dress, was carved from a three-ton block of Portland stone which was set upon a Purbeck stone base. The effigy was placed in St Martin's church in September 1939.

124. The War Memorial outside St Martin's church commemorates those men from the town and surrounding district who perished in the First World War. Various suggestions for a suitable memorial were put forward. In the summer of 1919 the town's choice of a cross of Purbeck stone set upon an octagonal base was erected at a cost of £400.

125.   An early photograph of North Street taken *c*.1868. Frederick Marshallsay had just opened his wine merchant and grocery business (right) and within two years the old Town Hall would be demolished. Cornelius Yearsley had recently taken over as landlord of the *Red Lion*; he initially brewed his own beer there and traded as a wine and spirit merchant.

126.   The lower part of North Street was completely re-built after the fire. By 1920, the properties on the right had been converted to business use. The National Provincial Bank of England had previously been the Dorsetshire Bank, established in 1830. The Post Office was next door—it opened in 1858 when it traded as a stamp office, stationer's, newsagent's and bookseller's.

127. The Old Filliter House, 1860. A large
block of land on the corner of North Street
and Dollins Lane was purchased by the
Filliters, who came to Wareham in 1715 and
established themselves as the borough's
leading Nonconformists. Various members
of this lawyer family served as town clerks
and mayors. Their rambling residence was
demolished in 1861.

128. 'St Martin's', the Filliter's Victorian mansion, was designed by Crickmay, the Weymouth architect. Built for Freeland Filliter, the house was the grandest residence in town. By 1935, it had been turned into an hotel and during the war was requisitioned by the army. Sold for £65,000 in 1973, it was demolished and replaced by a block of flats.

129. North Street, 1896. Centre right, the Wesleyan chapel nears completion; the adjoining manse for the minister is already occupied. On the extreme right is Glebe House, built in 1879 for Dr. Wudruffe Daniel, one of the town's two physicians. Custard's newsagency and refreshment rooms are on the left.

130. By 1848, Wesleyans were established in Wareham. In June 1896, the foundation stones of their new chapel and minister's house were laid by the mayor, Dr. Bell. Burt and Vick of Poole built the Gothic-style brick and Bath stone church which seated 350. In 1972 this building was demolished and replaced by a new Methodist church.

131. All Hallows', sited on the corner of Cow Lane and North Street, c.1870. This medieval building was originally a chapel-of-ease to the church of St Martin. It was sold in 1579 to a local landowner, then in 1774 converted into stables and afterwards into a warehouse and barn. It was demolished in the late 1880s.

132.   North Street, 1925. On the right, a pair of early 19th-century houses, Frank Christopher's shoe shop and the imposing large gabled, 'Glebe House'. Opposite, four bay-fronted dwellings were erected on the All Hallows site in 1887. Next door were the premises of Charles Fudge, a saddle and harness maker.

133.   J.A. Hobbs, 6 North Street, *c*.1900. In 1790, the town had two watchmakers. By 1885, Albert Hobbs advertised himself as a 'watchmaker, jeweller, gold and silversmith and optician'. He held a comprehensive stock of English, French and German watches and clocks as well as fancy jewellery. A Swiss watch sold for 5s. and a Hobbs 'celebrated Bean-Court' for 8s. 6d.

134. The Yews, 7 North Street, *c*.1910, with its
rendered front and iron railings; the latter were a
particular feature of North Street at the beginning of the
century. From about 1871-90, William Crocker, a linen-
draper, mercer, outfitter and general clothier, traded
there. After his retirement the family residence became
a boarding house.

135. The Yews, rear garden. Mrs. Elizabeth Crocker advertised 'Board and residence, a comfortable home from home in a charming old house and garden'. The Yews was one of the town's superior guest houses with comfort guaranteed and a garden set out for the enjoyment of guests. Aspidistras, the Victorians' favoured plant, are tastefully arranged on the flagstones.

136. Draper's, 7 North Street, c.1925. In the mid-1920s, Bessie Draper set up in business in a converted part of 'The Yews'. The house was drastically altered. The parapet, door porch and three windows were removed and replaced by a new shop front with bay window above. Although ownership changed, the shop continued as a ladies' and children's outfitters until the mid-1970s.

137. Edgar Custard senior had a newsagent's and refreshment rooms in West Street in 1885; 10 years later his son was established in North Street. The newsagency business expanded and by 1900 Mr. Custard was also an emigration agent arranging passages world-wide. He compiled and published the first comprehensive town guide, illustrated with picture postcards.

138. Frank Christopher, 22 North Street, traded from 1896-*c*.1923 and was one of five shoemakers in the town. Previously the premises had been the *Greyhound*, one of 16 pubs in Wareham in 1880. Earlier still, the *Greyhound* had been in succession, *The Crown, Royal Oak, Coach and Horses* and initially in 1801 *The Admiral Rodney*.

139. Junction of Cow Lane and North Street, *c.*1900. Left is 'Elm House', a much altered 16th-century building, re-fronted in the early 1800s. By 1902, Thomas and Edward Skewes ran the 'Elm House Academy for young gentlemen' there; the school was established in the 1840s on North Walls. Opposite, 'The Anglebury', one of the town's oldest dwellings, was built *c.*1600.

140. North Street, 1928. On the right, the Parkstone and Bournemouth Co-op came to Wareham just before 1923. (The 'Wareham Co-op' had traded in West Street in 1885.) Next door, Bessie Draper was now Bessie Ford and the family car is parked outside her shop. On the other side of the road, underneath the clock, was the town's first telephone box.

141.   North Street in the late 1940s. The street is cluttered with telegraph poles and telephone wires. Although the traffic was only moderate, parking on both sides of the road made driving rather hazardous. Frisby's shoe shop, extreme right, had opened just before 1923 and the Post Office, centre right, was newly built in 1936.

142.   Demolition of the Rainbow Café, 3 North Street, 1962. At the beginning of the century, 3 North Street was a private residence. By 1915, Bussey and Son, ladies' and gents' outfitters, had a flourishing business there. Mrs. Betty Monk converted the premises into 'Refreshment Rooms' in the early 1930s and specialised in luncheons, teas and homemade cakes.

143. Dugdale's, 45 North Street, *c.*1910. Charles Dugdale established his butcher's shop in the 1850s. Before refrigeration, meat was displayed inside and outside the premises in all weathers. The town's butchers were constantly reprimanded by the council for the state of their pig styes and slaughterhouses. Next door, George Wellstead traded as a china and glass dealer.

144. Mr. William Thomas is standing in the doorway of his tailor's shop at 55 North Street, *c.*1920. The cottages were built in the early 1800s and the shop window was a 20th-century alteration. The window display of a small number of gentlemen's suitings contrasts sharply with the over-filled shop windows of the previous years.

145. View down North Street, 1904. The cottages on the left (now demolished) were built in the late 1700s. Next to them is the enclosing wall of the Filliter property. The houses on the right date to the early 1800s. Mrs. Mary Sansom ran the grocery shop which was later taken over by William Bussell.

146. Top of North Street, late 1940s. Northover's garage was catering for an increasing demand for vehicle repairs and services. In 1840, John Elmes, coach maker, had started up in trade there. By 1900, Elmes were advertising 'motor cars painted and re-lined, carriages, carts and vans built to order'. The family-run business continued until the mid-1920s.

147. James Oliver Ford's cycle Depot at Coventry House, North Bridge, 1898. The Fords had been landlords of the *Lord Nelson* pub, which was opposite, since the 1840s. J.O. Ford opened his cycle shop in 1885 and the large house accommodated his growing family. Like many tradesmen of the time, he was actively involved in Town Council affairs.

148. North Mill was first recorded in 1150 when it belonged to the Prior of Wareham who received one tenth of all the grain processed there. In 1544, the mill was sold by Henry VIII to the Morton family of Milborne St Andrew. The substantial leat was probably dug either just before or just after the Norman conquest.

149. North Mill, 1900. In the early 1870s the buildings were used by Yeatman's of Poole, corn and seed merchants, but by 1878 the firm had withdrawn from trading in the town. The present buildings date to the 17th century but no doubt replaced earlier buildings on the same site.

150.   North Mill and North Bridge, 1900. The mill
buildings nestle at the base of North Walls; the little
bridge gave access to Wareham common. In the
background is the causeway and North Bridge. The
pointed left-hand arch is medieval; the other two
are round and date to 1670 when the bridge was re-
built.

151.   Originally part of the mill complex, 'Watts
Cottage' had been converted into a house by the
early 1900s and was occupied by a working-class
family. In 1891, 21 people were living in the four
dwellings around the mill, among them four
washerwomen. William Watts, a Northport farmer,
probably gave his name to the cottage.

152.   Baggs Mill, *c.*1920, is upstream of North Mill on the river Piddle. It has also been known as West Mill and Wareham Mill. Paper was manufactured there from the 1600s to 1830. Shortly afterwards the Baggs took it over and milled (and farmed) there for several generations. The 18th-century buildings were converted into flats in the 1980s.

153.   North Causeway, the main road out of town to Poole and Bere Regis, *c.*1910. Elm Villas, overlooking the river Piddle, were built in 1896 for Mr. J.O. Ford, owner of Coventry House (centre). Part of the North Causeway and North Bridge were in Morden parish, part in St Martin's parish and both parishes shared the expense of upkeep and repairs.

154.   Northport, *c*.1905. (Photograph by Fred Hibbs.) The hamlet, first mentioned in 1370, is just north of Wareham. Far left is the *Railway Inn*. Before 1847 it had been known as *The Country House*. On the right is Fred Hibbs' shop. For many years he was the Northport baker and at the turn of the century also ran a sub-post office.

155.   The railway crossing, *c*.1920. By the 1950s, the crossing was causing traffic bottlenecks due to the frequency of the trains and the increased number of vehicles on the road. Centre left is the *Railway Inn*. When it was built in the early 1800s it was sited to take advantage of the Turnpike road traffic.

156.   This Adams '442' Tank engine was built in the 1880s and operated on the Wareham to Swanage branch line. The photograph was taken between 1910 and 1923 when the coaches had their distinctive London and South Western livery of salmon and pink. The train, which stopped at Corfe Castle, had two coaches and a guard's van.

157.   The brick-built goods shed was part of the original railway layout and was erected in 1847. Brown and Son operated their haulage business there for a short time after the First World War. Mr. and Mrs. Brown pose with staff and the company vehicles, which bridge the gap between horse-drawn and motorised transport.

158. The Dorset Quarry Company's site was just north of the railway station. Purbeck stone was brought in by waggons from the quarries near Swanage and then worked at the yard. The finished stone was loaded directly onto goods trains and taken to London to be used in building work in the city. The company closed in 1930.

159. Buller's Army at Wareham station, August 1898. General Sir Redvers Buller led the last manoeuvres with 25,000 troops at Wareham, before the army embarked for South Africa and the Boer War. The railway line had been completed in 1847 but the station was re-built in 1864, up-line and west of its original site.

160. The 7th Field Co. Royal Engineers prepare to march to camp. The arrival of such enormous numbers of troops demanded elaborate liaison between the railway authorities and the army to interrupt normal services as little as possible. In the background are the gatekeeper's cottages and the station goods yard.

161. The troops march with military precision to Trigon, one mile north of the station. Their equipment was brought to camp by waggons. The camp was laid out by the Royal Engineers who erected temporary buildings and constructed a field telegraph system. The Tollhouse (centre) was sited on the Wareham exit of the Poole Turnpike road.

162. This photograph was specially arranged and produced by photographer William Churchill to commemorate the 'Relief of Ladysmith', by Sir Redvers Buller on 28 February 1900, during the Boer War. The town's worthies are discussing the receipt of the official telegram outside the Post Office. The street and houses are suitably decorated with flags and bunting.

163.   Sandford House was described as 'an elegant mansion of white brick with stone dressings in Elizabethan style'. The estate of 1,500 acres, overlooking Poole Harbour, was surrounded by fir plantations. The house, two miles from Wareham, was built for the Rodgett brothers, Miles and Richard, in 1860. The family, mill owners from Preston (Lancashire), came south for health reasons.

164.   Heath Cottages were built by the Rodgetts for their staff. They employed household servants as well as a large number of estate workers. The cottages imitated the style of the mansion both in the brickwork and window shapes. The family were good and generous employers and great benefactors to both the parish church and the town.

165. Army Cadet and General Training Corps at the Senior School, 1942. Captain 'Bill' Stuckey, headmaster of the school, formed the Corps on 11 May 1942 to help prepare young men for the armed services. They met weekly, practised drill, performed manoeuvres and mock battles and were issued with uniforms and equipment by the Government. The unit was disbanded in 1945.

166.   Girls of the Land Army outside the Y.M.C.A. at Victoria House, Howard's Lane, 1942. The girls, who came from all over England, were billeted at Victoria House. They were taken by lorry to the Purbeck countryside, where they assisted in such duties as cutting and burning brushwood, clearing undergrowth and cutting pit props.

167. In 1945, Wareham welcomed back its young men who had been away on active service during the war. A grand dinner was organised by Mr. and Mrs. Yates, landlord and landlady of the *Duke of Wellington* in East Street. The slap up meal took place in the Corn Exchange at the Town Hall.

168. 'The First Elizabeth' was performed by the pupils of the County Modern School to celebrate the coronation of Queen Elizabeth in 1953. The town enjoyed festivities on a lavish scale. They included a civic service, exhibition, treats for the children, dancing, the coronation film at the Rex and culminated in a grand banquet at the end of September.

169.   Thomas Pride was awarded the V.C. in 1865 for 'Conspicuous gallantry' during an attack on the Straits of Simonsaki, Japan. Captain of the afterguard, he sustained injuries which ended his naval career. Born near South Bridge in 1835, he was in his latter years a toll-gate keeper and for a time lived at Sandford. He died in 1893.

170. The first school in Wareham was noted in 1700. By 1888, when school attendance became compulsory, the new church school was only three years old. Mrs. Rodgett of Sandford had funded the school building which replaced the cramped and outdated facilities at Holy Trinity church. The school photo is from 1952 when Mr. Thorne was headmaster.

171. Lloyd's Bank, South Street. In 1762, the 'Fire of Wareham' started here in the back garden of the *Bull's Head Inn*. Two thirds of the town was destroyed in one afternoon and Wareham, as depicted in the preceding pages, owes its subsequent development to the events of that fateful day.

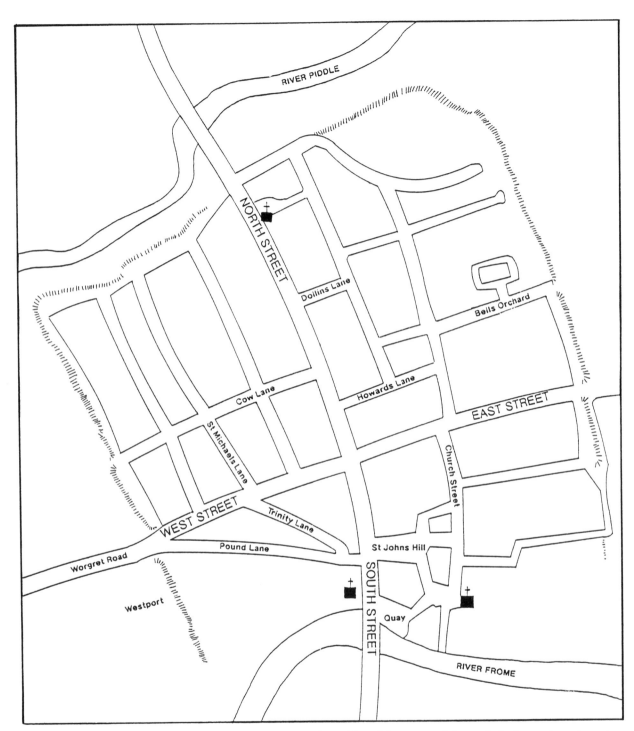

172. Streets and lanes mentioned in the text. The walls on three sides of the town and the castle in the south-west quarter have dictated the street pattern. The narrow back lanes are a strong feature of Wareham, their names indicative of occupational associations, vanished features and some of the people who lived there.

WAREHAM
✻ PARISH ✠ MAGAZINE. ✻

No. 305.　　　　　**MAY, 1909.**　　　　　**[PRICE 1d.**

CLERGY.

RECTOR : REV. SELWYN BLACKETT, The Rectory.

CURATES .　{ REV. F. W. PEVERELLE.

CHURCHWARDENS.

ST. MARY.	ST. MARTIN.
Mr. G. E. Paul, West Street.	Mr. Jas. Speed, North Street.
Mr. E. J. Sansom, South Street.	Mr. C. G. Shaw, Sandford.
HOLY TRINITY.	**ARNE.**
Mr. W. J. Randall, West Street.	Mr. G. H. Candy, Arne.
Mr. J. S. Burr, South Street.	Mr. R. E. Pinney, Arne.

ORGANIST : MR. C. E. WOOD.

SCRIPTURE READER : Mr. WILLIAM BEARDSLEY, 5, Bestwall Villas.

VERGER : Mr. SCUTT, North Street.

This Magazine can be obtained at Mr. H. Snelling's, North Street, Wareham; at Miss Kelsey's, South Street, Wareham; or it can be sent by post on application to the Editor.

W. S. HALLETT, GENERAL PRINTER, MARKET PLACE, POOLE.